JOSH COHEN
RADIOHEAD
FOR SOLO PIANO

Dedicated to:
Aviva & Joel
Tali, Nellie & Danny
Margot & Rafael
Faye & Mervyn
Jeremy

Special thanks:
Danny Cohen
Aimee Chapman, Jade Roberts, Aurélie Casrouge
Tristan Ceddia at Never Now, Benjamin Sexton, Warren Lain
Grace Cloney, James Ball and everyone at the Josh Cohen School of Music
Tony Grujovski at Studio Legal, r/Radiohead, all of my YouTube fans
Werner Wolff, Andrew Okrzeja and João Pais at Notengrafik Berlin
Dave Havea, Andy Reed, Pat Moevasa-Sili, Colin Leadbetter
Bryce Edge, Lucy Holliday and Oliver Weeks

Arranged and transcribed by Josh Cohen
'Paranoid Android' transcribed by Oliver Weeks
Artwork by Stanley Donwood, 'Twisted Wood Series'
Author photograph by Danny Cohen
Edited by Lucy Holliday
Designed by Dominic Brookman

© 2019 by Faber Music Ltd
First published by Faber Music Ltd in 2019
Bloomsbury House
74–77 Great Russell Street
London WC1B 3DA
Printed in England by Caligraving Ltd
All rights reserved

ISBN10: 0-571-54105-4
EAN13: 978-0-571-54105-8

Reproducing this music in any form is illegal
and forbidden by the Copyright, Designs and Patents Act, 1988

To buy Faber Music publications or to find out about the full range of titles available,
please contact your local music retailer or Faber Music sales enquiries:

Faber Music Limited, Burnt Mill, Elizabeth Way, Harlow CM20 2HX
Tel: + 44 (0)1279 82 89 82   Fax: + 44 (0)1279 82 89 83
sales@fabermusic.com   fabermusicstore.com

07 DAYDREAMING
14 EVERYTHING IN ITS RIGHT PLACE
26 NO SURPRISES
34 EXIT MUSIC (FOR A FILM)
40 SAIL TO THE MOON
46 KARMA POLICE
54 PYRAMID SONG
62 CODEX
67 VIDEOTAPE
76 TRUE LOVE WAITS
81 PARANOID ANDROID

BIOGRAPHY

Josh Cohen is a pianist residing in Melbourne, Australia.

More than a decade of classical tuition that later diverged into jazz and improvisation underscores Josh's sound and playing but it is the space, simplicity and intensity of emotion that fundamentally drive his arrangements and compositions.

Josh found musical solace from the competing constraints of his training through a meditative and highly improvised approach to playing some of his favourite songs in endlessly evolving and creative ways. This exploration was the impetus for his YouTube channel, where he has presented idiosyncratic covers of Radiohead, Pink Floyd, Sigur Rós and David Bowie.

Josh consistently embarks into unknown territory despite the familiarity of the songs, and it is this combination of comfort and surprise that has resonated with listeners, garnering millions of views and instigating deeply personal commentary from listeners around the globe.

In 2019, Josh is releasing this songbook, will embark on a number of live performances and his original band Auto Luna will debut the first single from their forthcoming album. As to future projects, he is letting things unfold via the strange alchemy of hard work and serendipity that has guided his journey so far.

INTRODUCTION

This has to be one of the most surreal moments in my life. As a teenager I fumbled my way through songbooks just like this one, my playing bearing little resemblance to the sheet music whatsoever and now, here I am writing an introduction for my own publication of improvised solo piano Radiohead arrangements. Man, life is weird sometimes. Here's how it all began.

My journey kicked off when I was seven years old playing around with some musical memory games on a 1987 Vtech Smart Start "interactive pre-computer learning machine". This inspired me to ask my parents to borrow a tiny two-octave keyboard from their friends, which led me to start having lessons with an old-school Russian piano teacher called Julian every Wednesday afternoon. I was a useless student. My practice routine consisted of last-minute run-throughs of repertoire from really dated tutor books half an hour before he arrived — a true procrastinator at work. Being an emotional cat didn't help as well, so if you speak to my mum, she'll recall the countless times I ended up in tears every lesson. I only wanted to play music that I recognised, as the concept of playing a piece of music that I hadn't heard or read before scared the bejesus out of me.

At thirteen, along came a Roland digital piano courtesy of my parents and grandparents and I met an absolute sweetheart of a piano teacher in Mrs Moloney, who guided me through the classical examination system throughout my secondary education. Whilst I actually enjoyed the lessons, I counteracted the strict discipline of classical training with an abundance of pop songbooks that I never really mastered and managed to fail grade four and grade five theory in the process. I knew I loved playing the instrument but after finishing high school and struggling my way through music, I needed a breather.

Whilst studying an arbitrary double degree in Business and Computing, I randomly sat at a grand piano in the middle of a shopping centre and played. I came back to that piano every weekend, unpaid but unencumbered, for the next couple of years and the music came back too. Lessons with jazz pianist Steve Sedergreen helped get my head around jazz piano and introduced me to improvisation, not something that I had a general knack for, but after twelve years of classical training, certainly a healthy curiosity. Thankfully, Spencer, a close friend of mine, took it upon himself to shake me violently until I dropped out of my degrees and pursued music.

I studied Jazz and Improvisation and adored the degree and the vibe of the course — I had found my niche. I studied some fascinating subjects, started collaborating with Dave, Andy and Pat, musical friendships that have evolved into the original band Auto Luna and I rapidly learned more about the piano than I had ever learned before. In my last year of studies, I wigged out about the uncertain future of a classically and jazz trained musician. I started teaching piano in students' homes to compensate, took the plunge to secure a loan to purchase the very piano most of you may have seen on my YouTube channel, and opened up a small piano school.

Countless times during lessons my students would show me pianists on YouTube playing covers, often with millions of views and recorded fairly poorly. Every now and then when I could find a spare moment on a Sunday afternoon, I thought that I could perhaps record a few small improvisations over tunes that I was digging to showcase my school. I honestly thought nothing of it at the time, but as I continued to post videos, along came views and subscribers in the boatloads. I received some heartfelt messages from people all around the world who were listening in to the channel and there were persistent requests for sheet music of the performances. I continually had to explain to everyone that the sheet music simply didn't exist on paper, as they were just arrangements of me playing whatever I was feeling in the moment. Eventually I was left with no choice but to start notating a selection of Radiohead arrangements from the YouTube channel.

It has been a challenging and arduous process transcribing and arranging these tracks. Converting the analogue nature of playing improvised piano arrangements into the very rigid grid of digital notation has its limitations. It's even more perplexing to think about converting this information back into an analogue feel for you to replicate my style of piano playing on your own instrument. Given the amount of improvised elements in the arrangements, there was always going to be some information that was lost in translation due to the constraints of Western notation. For example, I couldn't find a musical symbol to indicate a "reverse accent" — to play an individual note softer than the rest of the surrounding notes, so you'll see these noteheads are slightly smaller to give them less emphasis. Combining the melody and accompaniment in the right hand requires some careful consideration to differentiate the two, so I chose to split up the voices in the treble clef and include lyrics to indicate where the melody lies — make sure you bring the melody out over the accompaniment to get the full effect. Certain tracks require an emphasis on the backbeat such as 'Karma Police', 'Sail to the Moon' and the chorus of 'Exit Music (For a Film)'. There are also some interesting time signature choices that may feel somewhat unusual and unconventional, but I hope that it will give you a clearer insight into how I approach the feel of these tunes in my head.

Before diving into these arrangements, I'd suggest that you don't interpret these charts literally. I know this may be challenging to some players, but the end goal should be to have some flexibility and creative freedom to use these arrangements as a template and guide, rather than diligently reading every note dot-to-dot. They weren't arranged to be played exactly as written, nor should they be played that way when replicating them.

Regardless of whether you're staring down the barrel of your first songbook, a professional who can read these notes better than I can, or anywhere in between, I genuinely hope you find some inspiration and beauty from playing these arrangements.

Josh Cohen

Daydreaming

Words and Music by Thomas Yorke, Philip Selway
Edward O'Brien, Colin Greenwood and Jonathan Greenwood
Arrangement and transcription by Josh Cohen

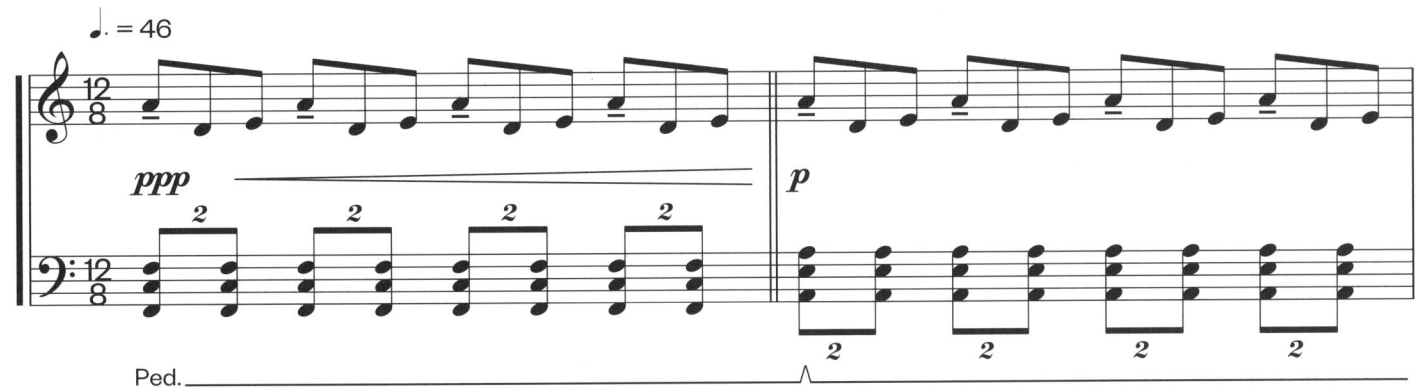

© 2016 Warner/Chappell Music Ltd
All Rights Reserved.

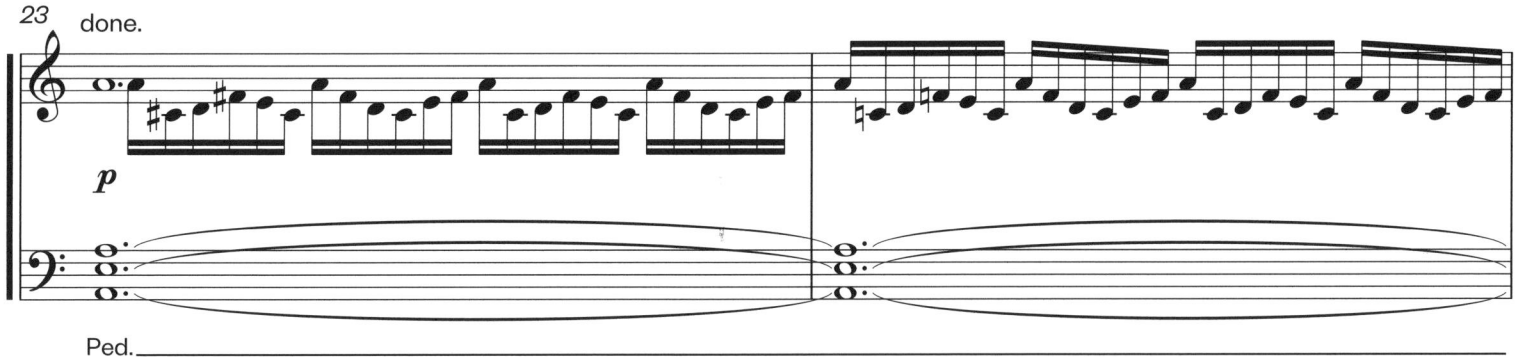
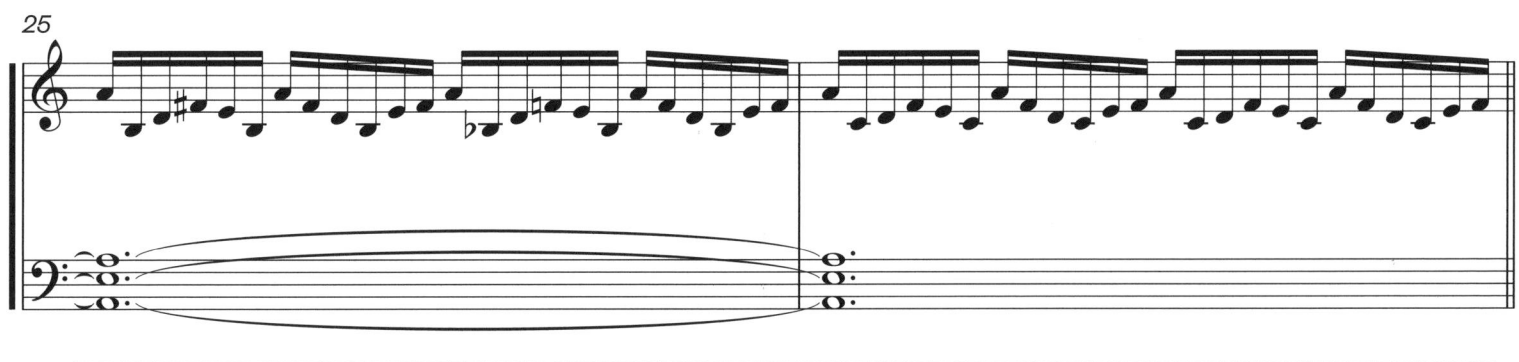
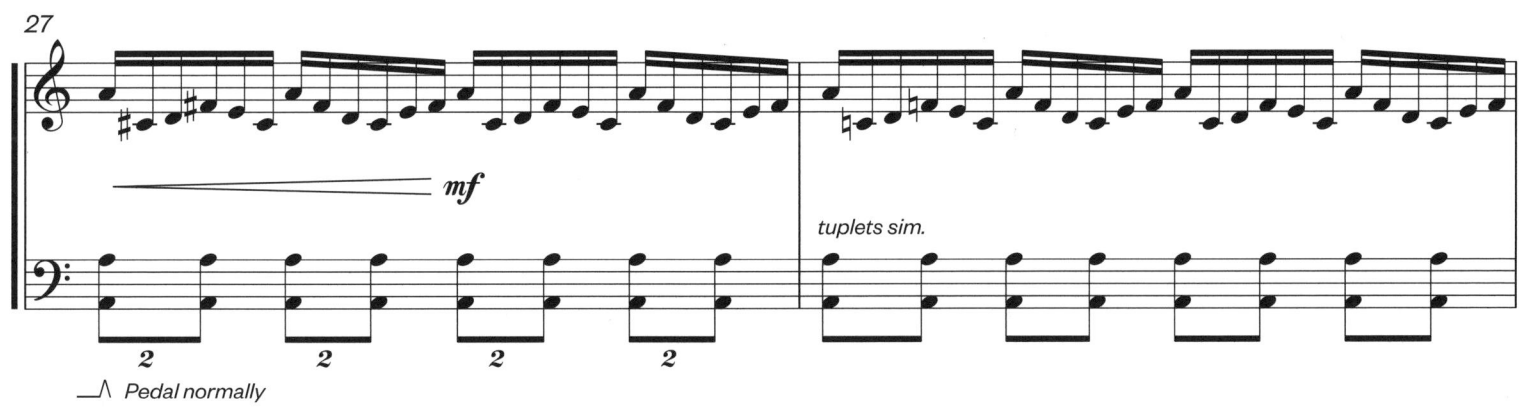

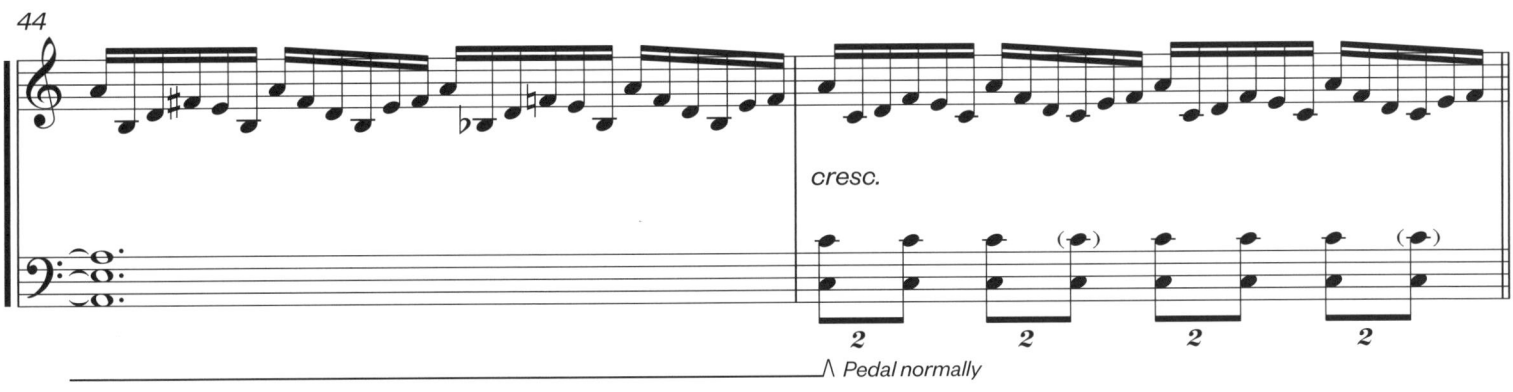
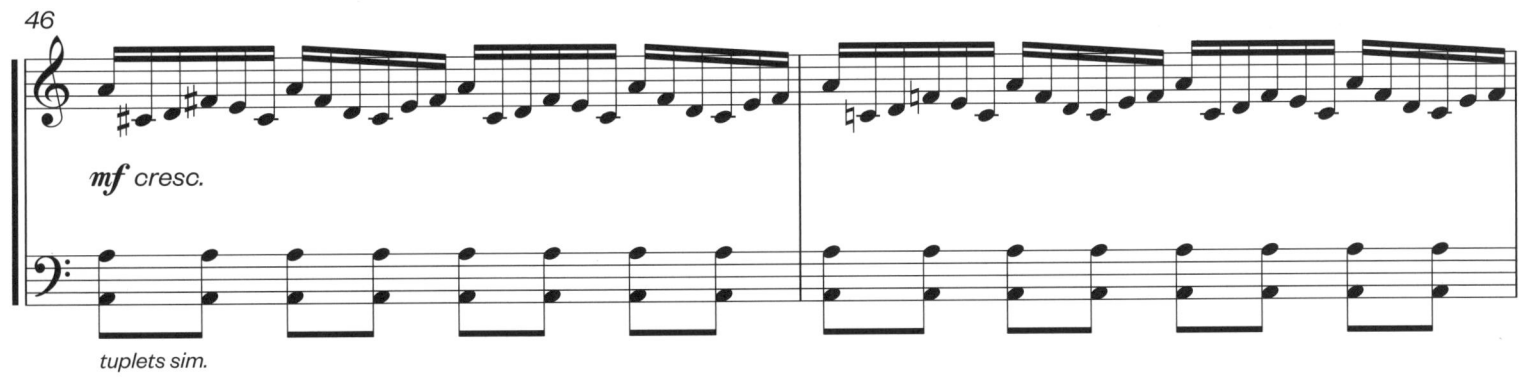

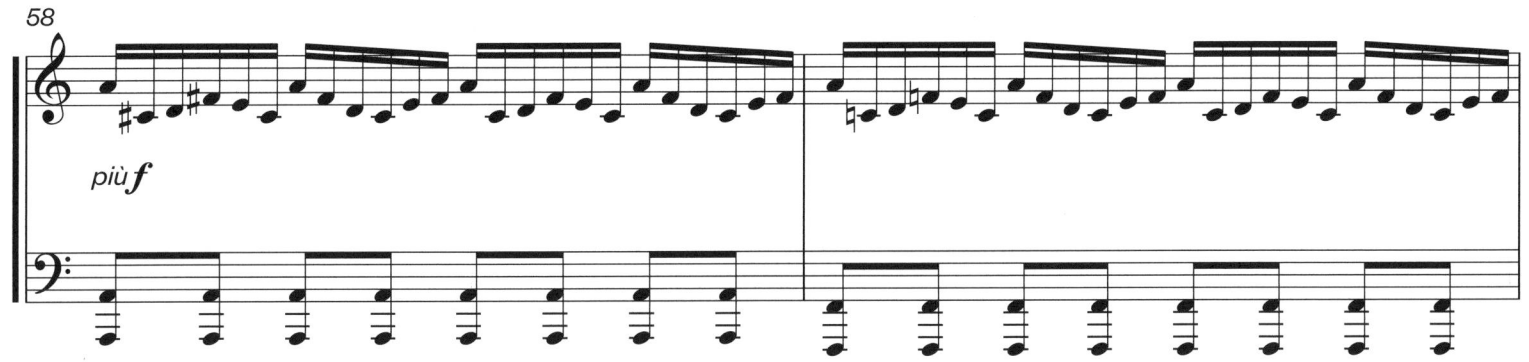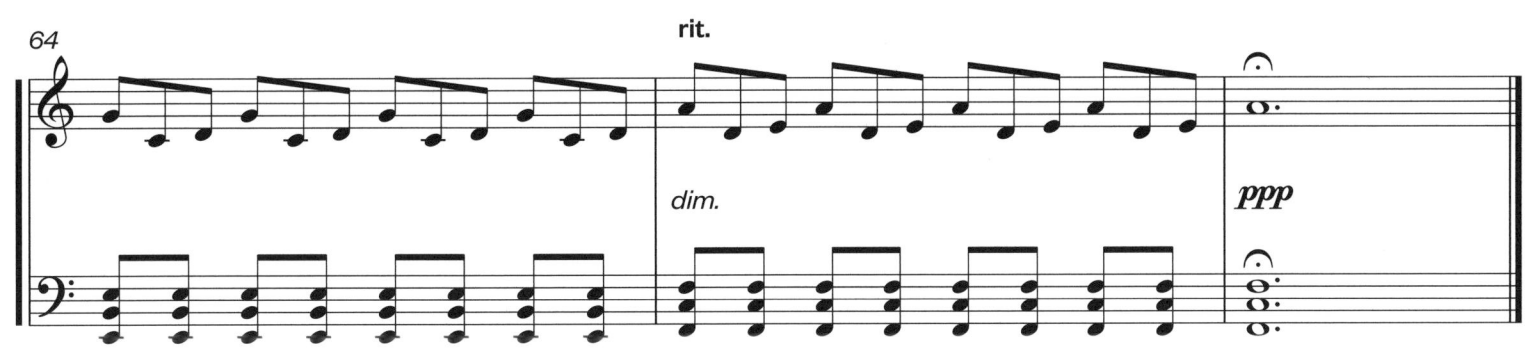

Everything In Its Right Place

Words and Music by Thomas Yorke, Philip Selway,
Edward O'Brien, Colin Greenwood and Jonathan Greenwood
Arrangement and transcription by Josh Cohen

© 2000 Warner/Chappell Music Ltd
All Rights Reserved.

No Surprises

Words and Music by Thomas Yorke, Philip Selway,
Edward O'Brien, Colin Greenwood and Jonathan Greenwood
Arrangement and transcription by Josh Cohen

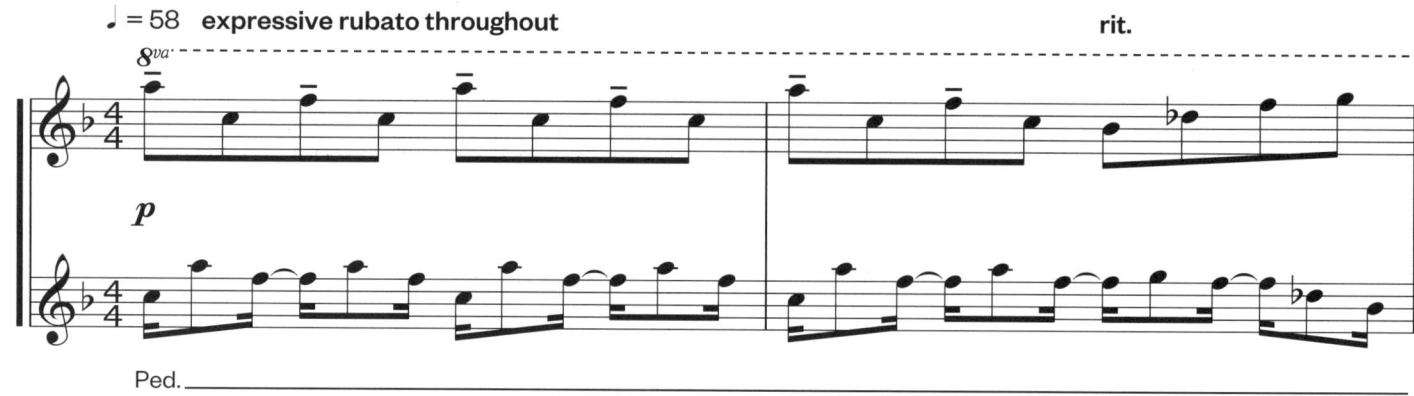
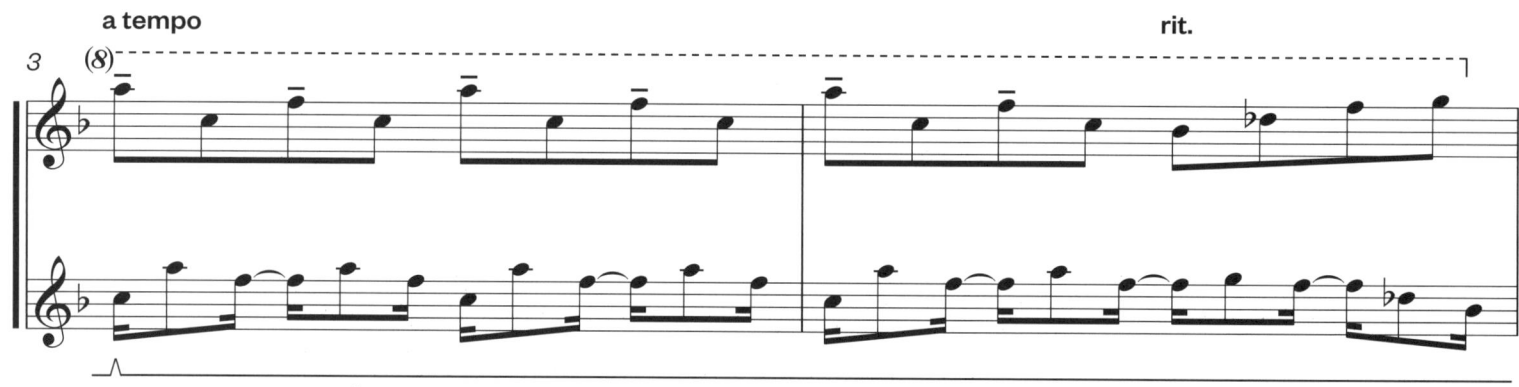

© 1997 Warner/Chappell Music Ltd
All Rights Reserved.

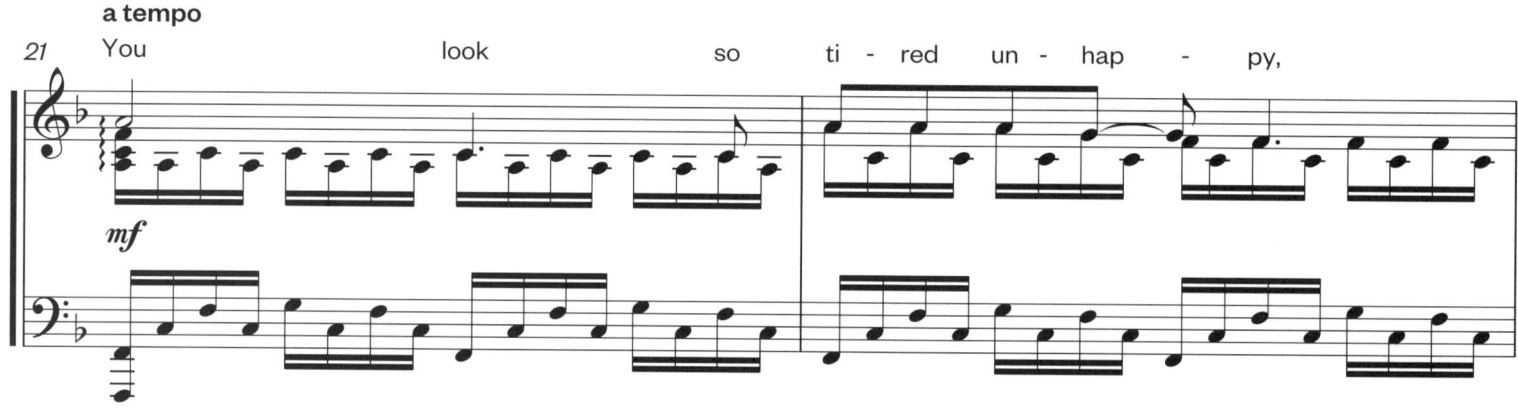
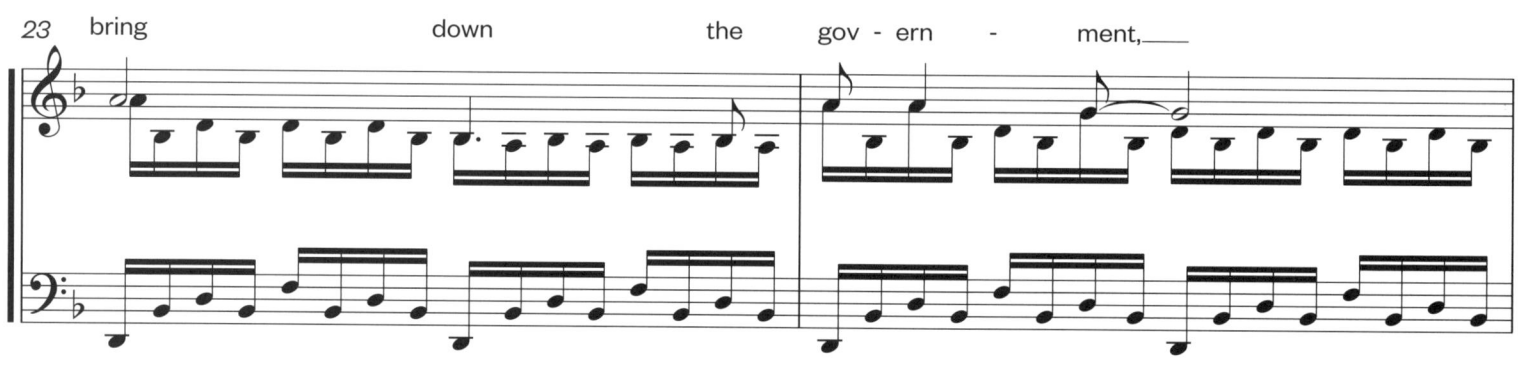

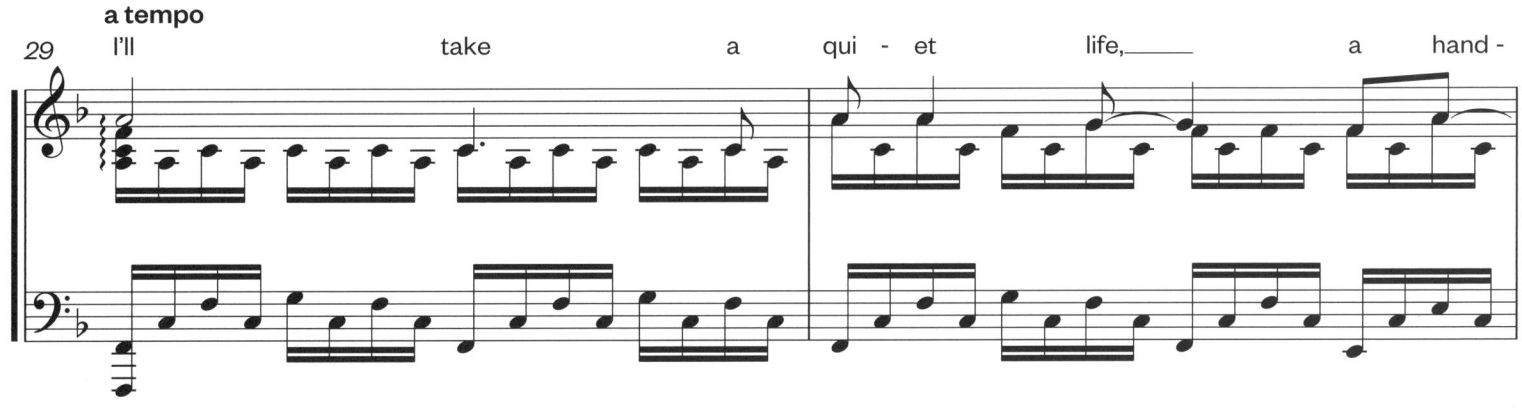
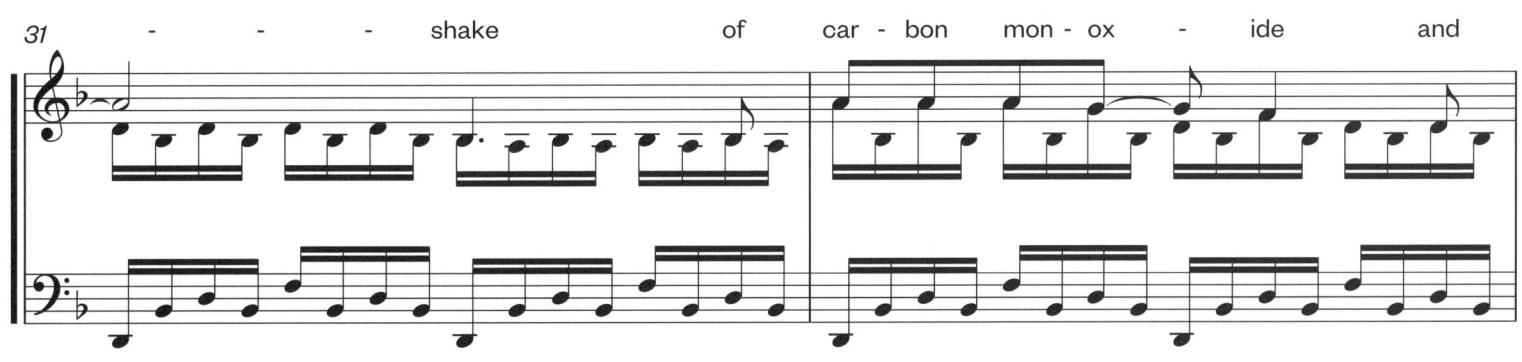
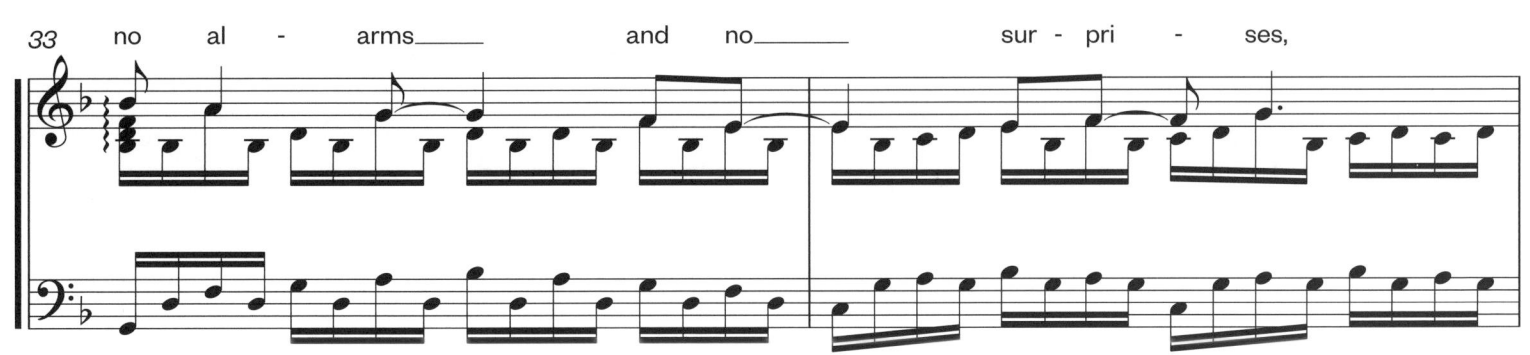

Exit Music (For A Film)

Words and Music by Thomas Yorke, Philip Selway,
Edward O'Brien, Colin Greenwood and Jonathan Greenwood
Arrangement and transcription by Josh Cohen

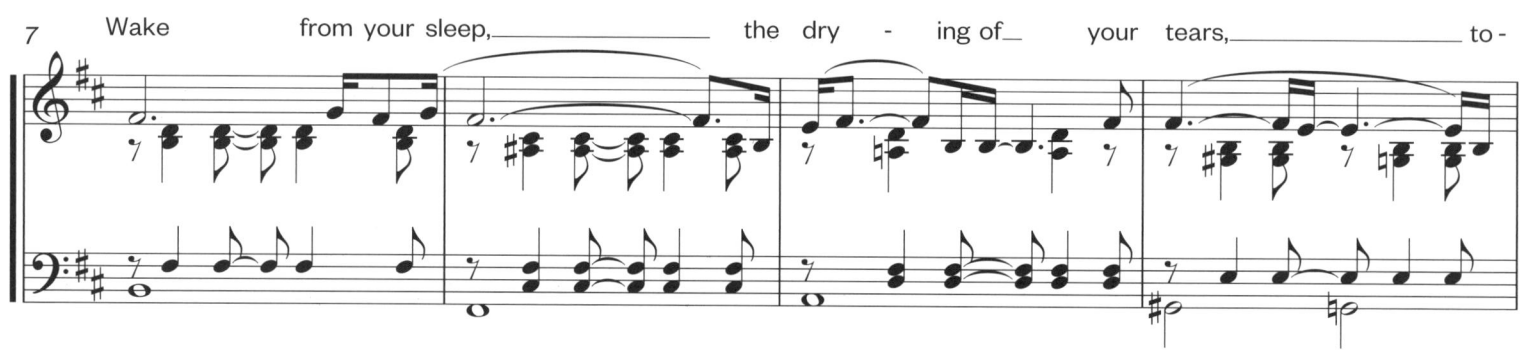

© 1997 Warner/Chappell Music Ltd
All Rights Reserved.

Sail To The Moon

Words and Music by Thomas Yorke, Philip Selway,
Edward O'Brien, Colin Greenwood and Jonathan Greenwood
Arrangement and transcription by Josh Cohen

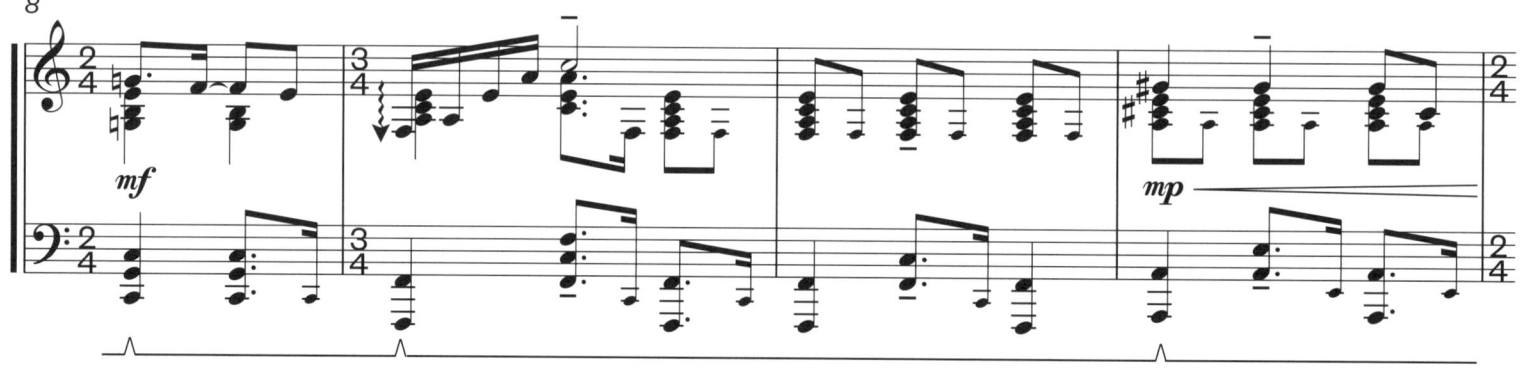
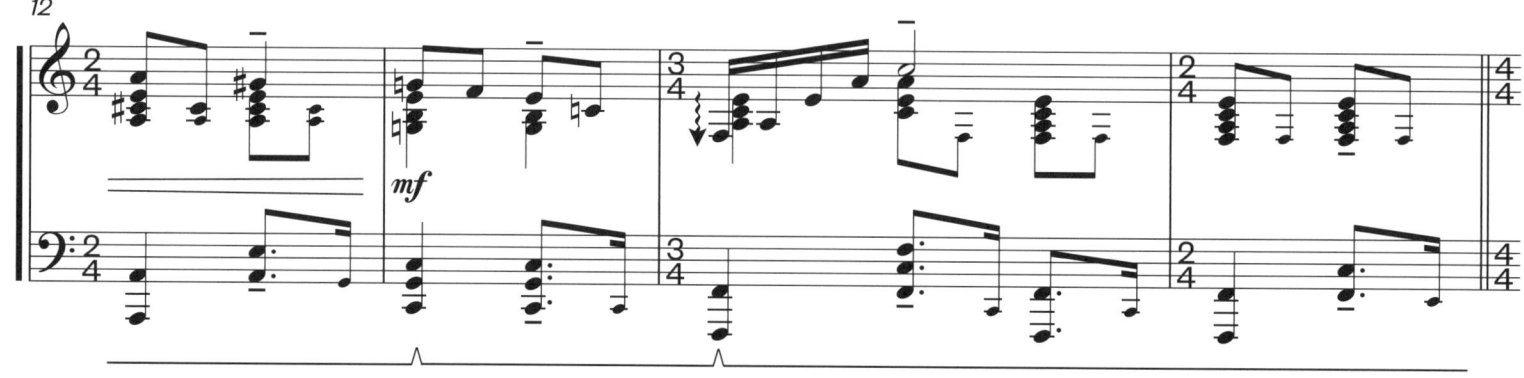

© 2002 Warner/Chappell Music Ltd
All Rights Reserved.

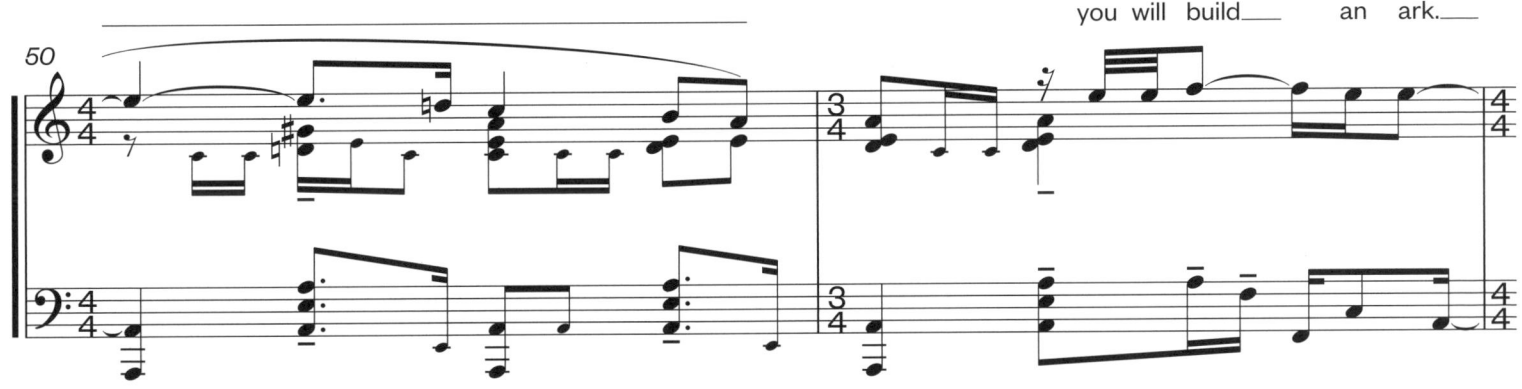

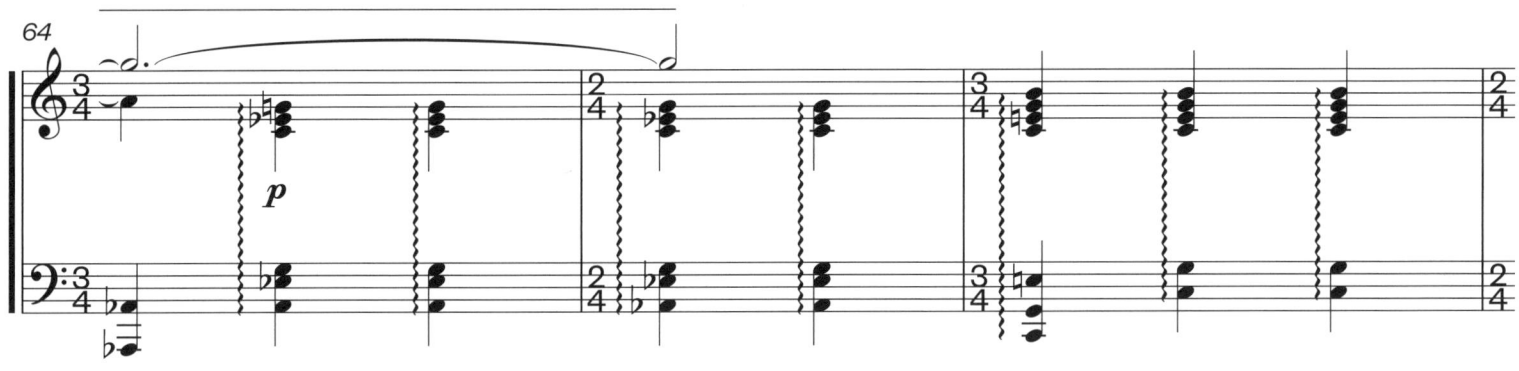
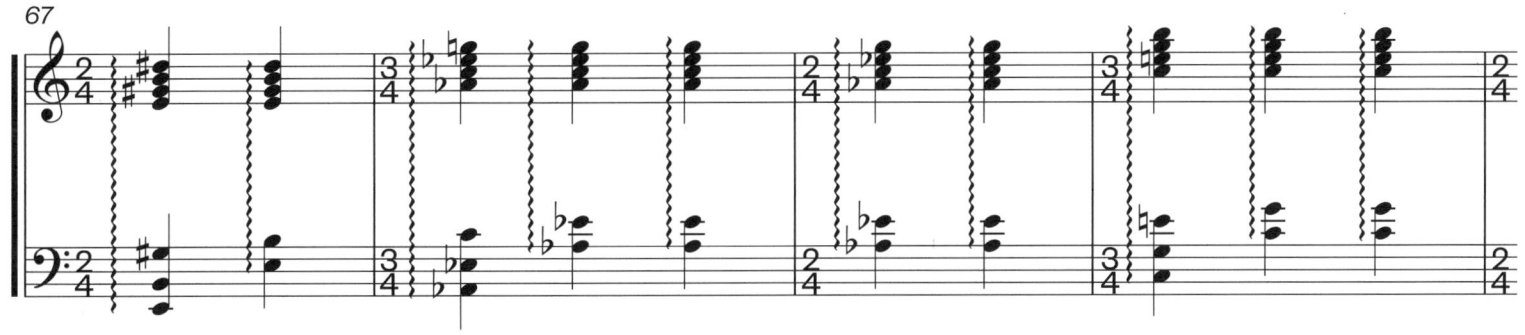
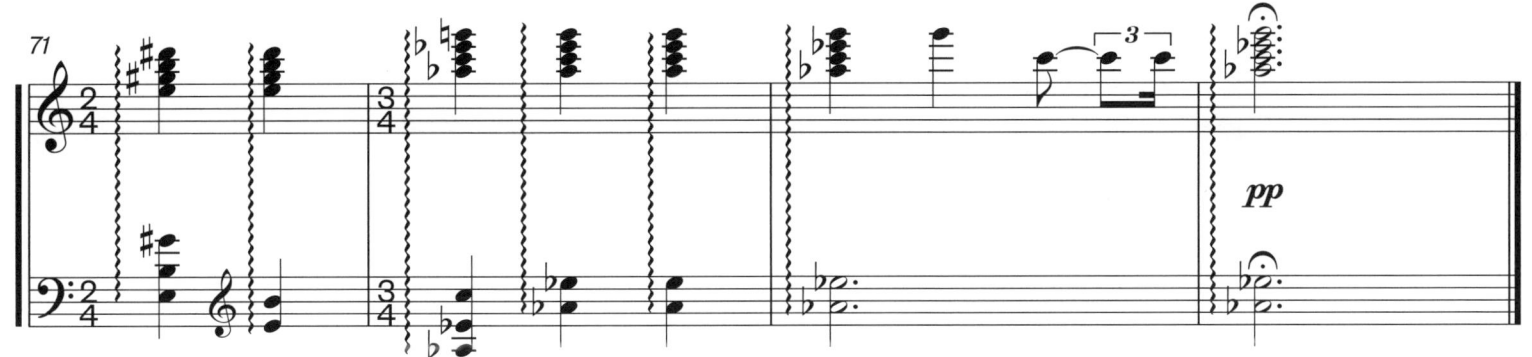

Karma Police

Words and Music by Thomas Yorke, Jonathan Greenwood, Colin Greenwood, Edward O'Brien and Philip Selway
Arrangement and transcription by Josh Cohen

© 1997 Warner/Chappell Music Ltd
All Rights Reserved.

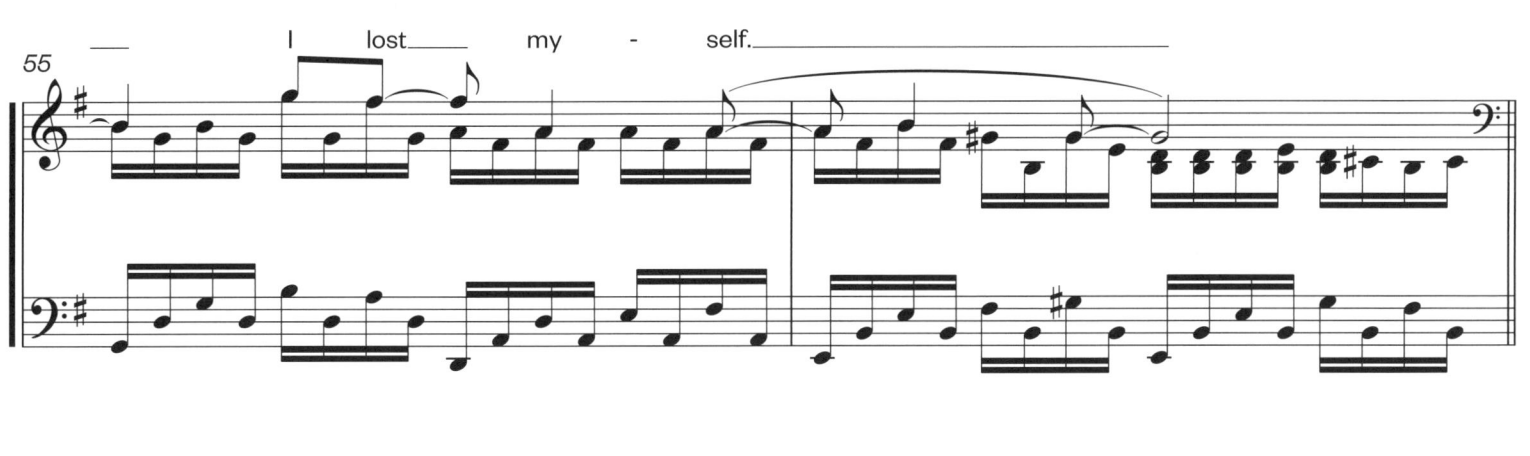

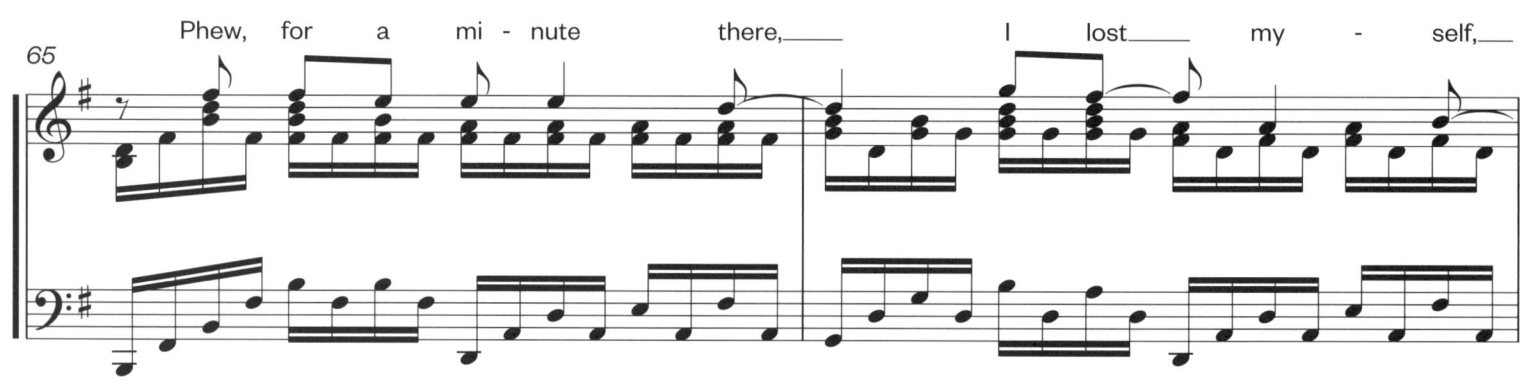
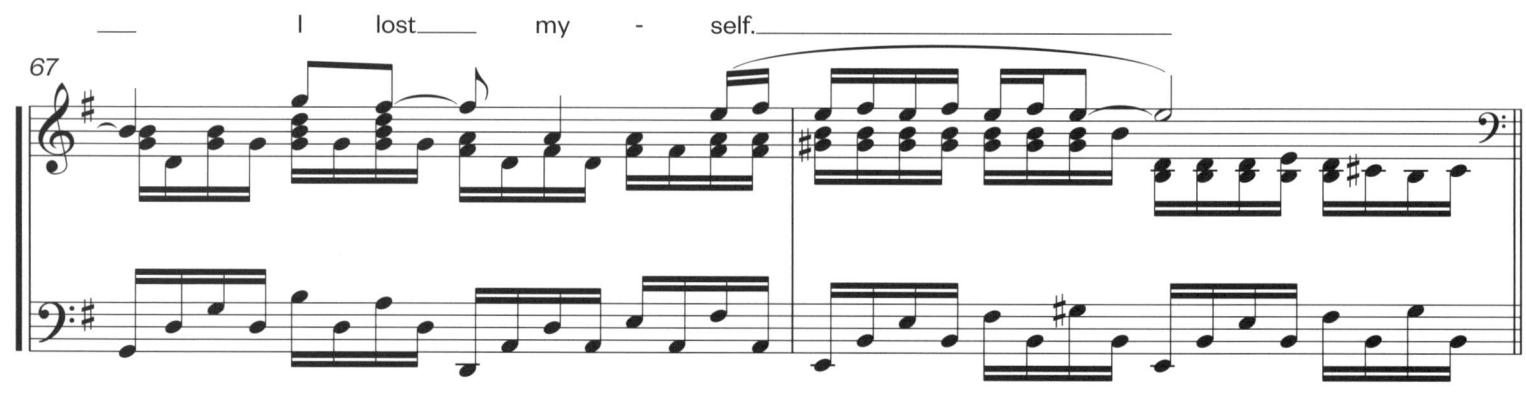

Pyramid Song

Words and Music by Thomas Yorke, Jonathan Greenwood,
Colin Greenwood, Edward O'Brien and Philip Selway
Arrangement and transcription by Josh Cohen

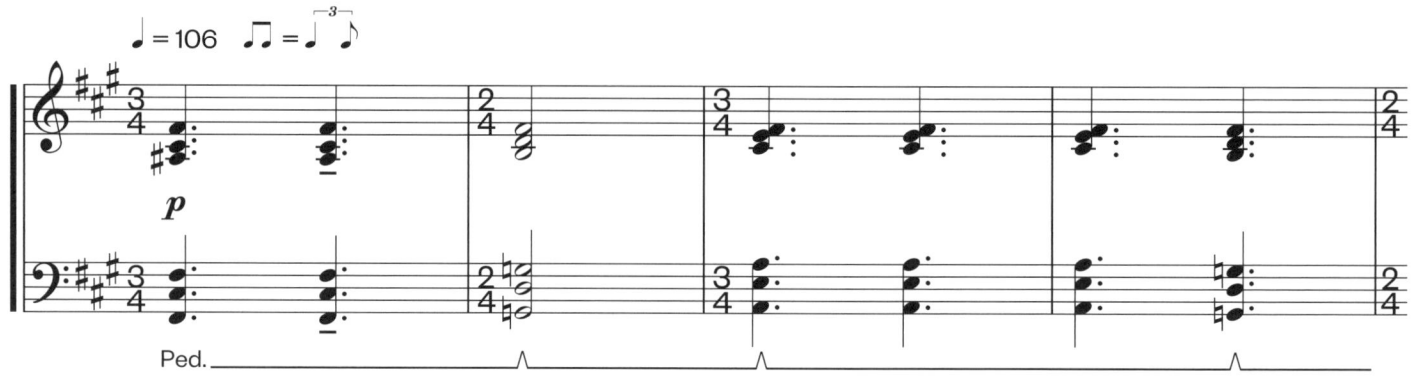

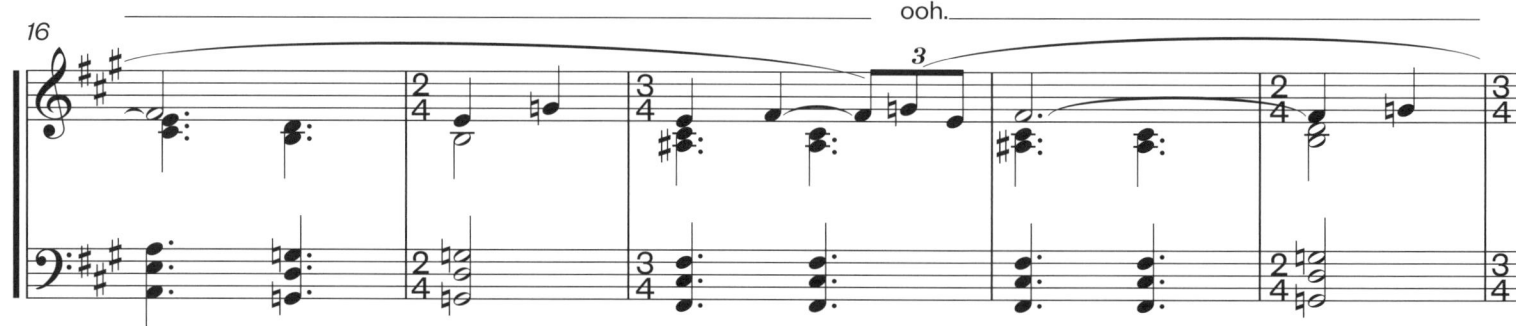

© 2001 Warner/Chappell Music Ltd
All Rights Reserved.

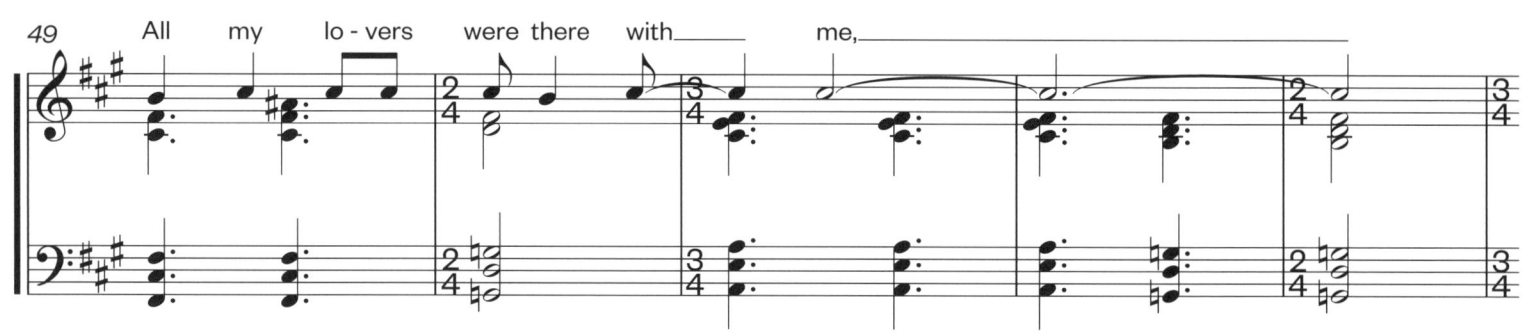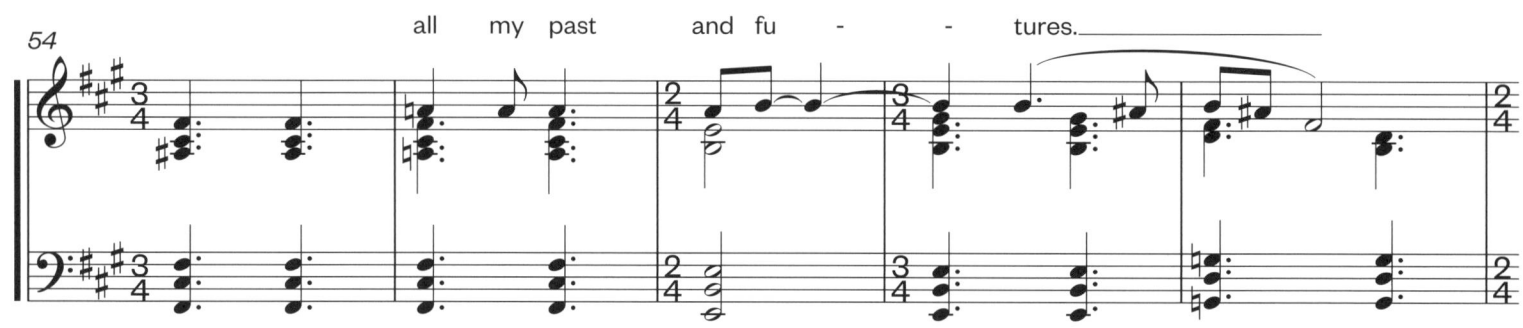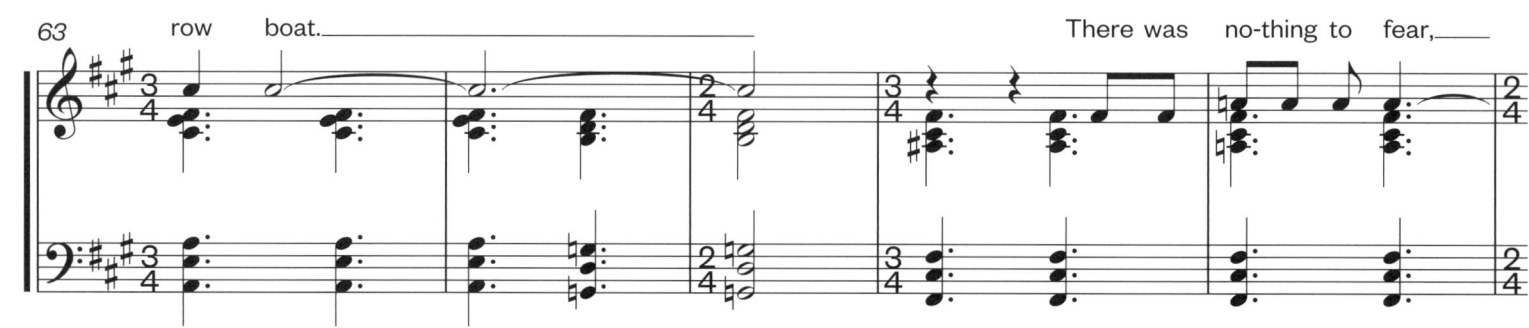

Codex

Words and Music by Thomas Yorke, Jonathan Greenwood,
Colin Greenwood, Edward O'Brien and Philip Selway
Arrangement and transcription by Josh Cohen

© 2011 Warner/Chappell Music Ltd
All Rights Reserved.

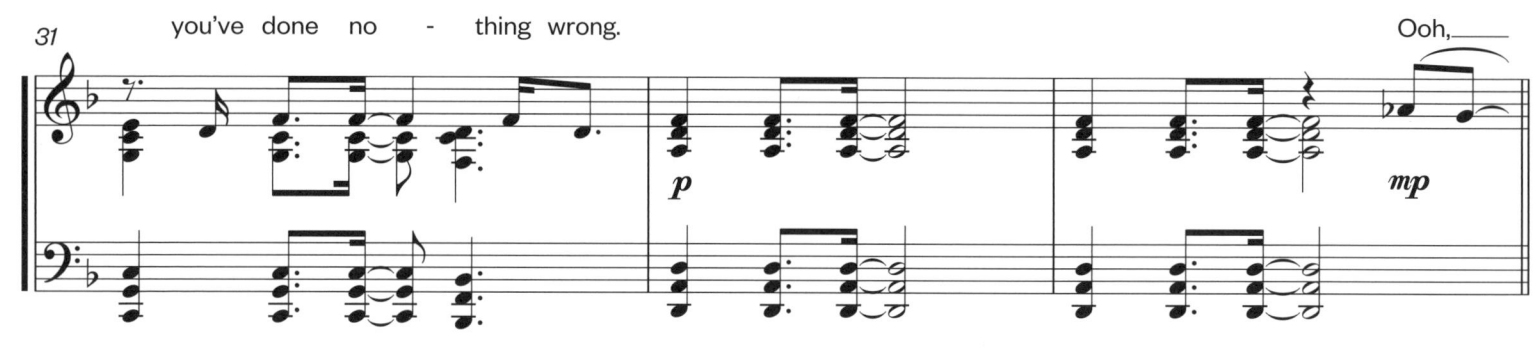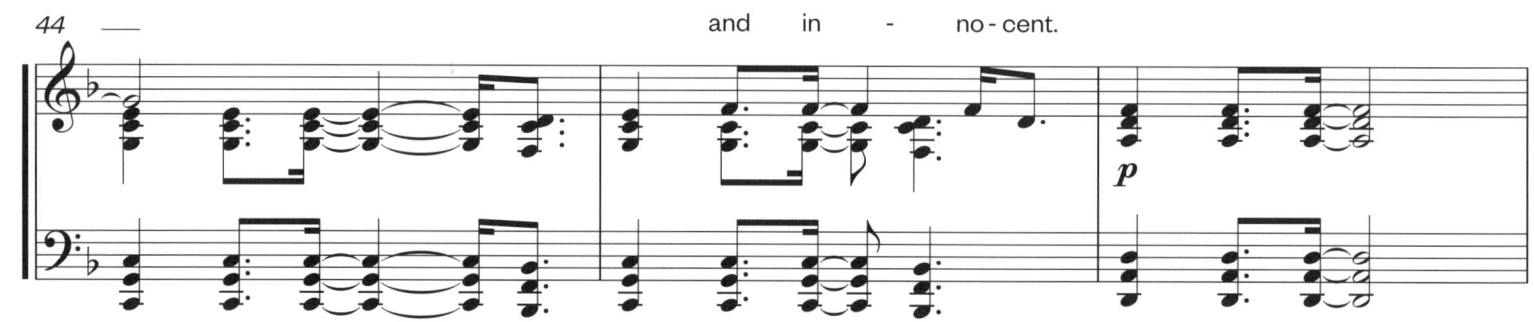

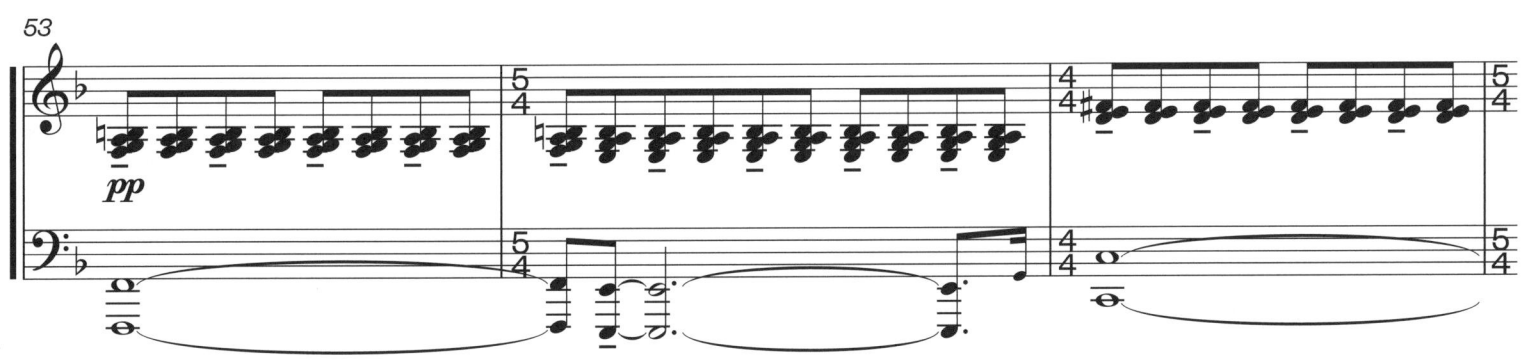

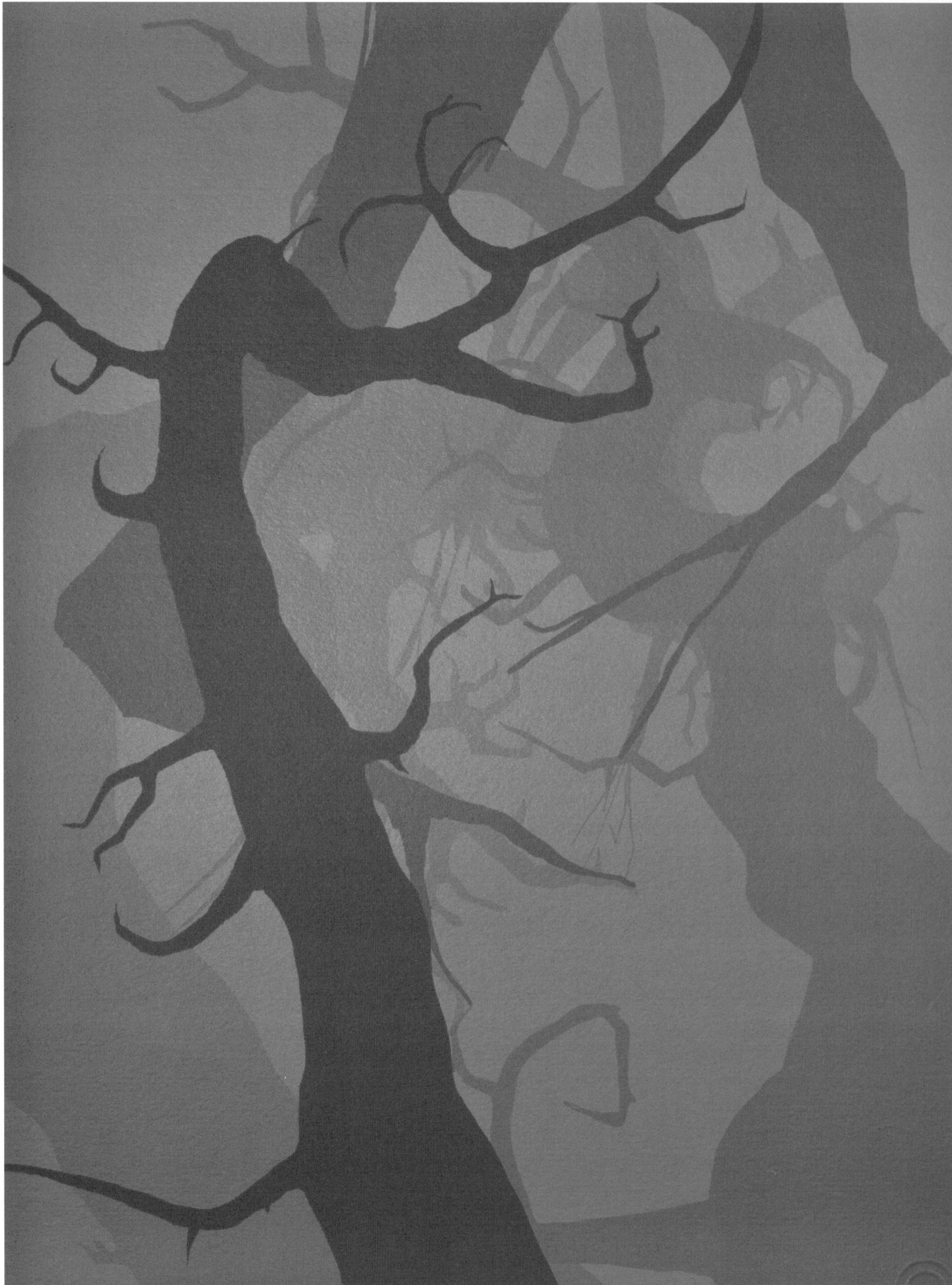

Videotape

Words and Music by Thomas Yorke, Jonathan Greenwood,
Colin Greenwood, Edward O'Brien and Philip Selway
Arrangement and transcription by Josh Cohen

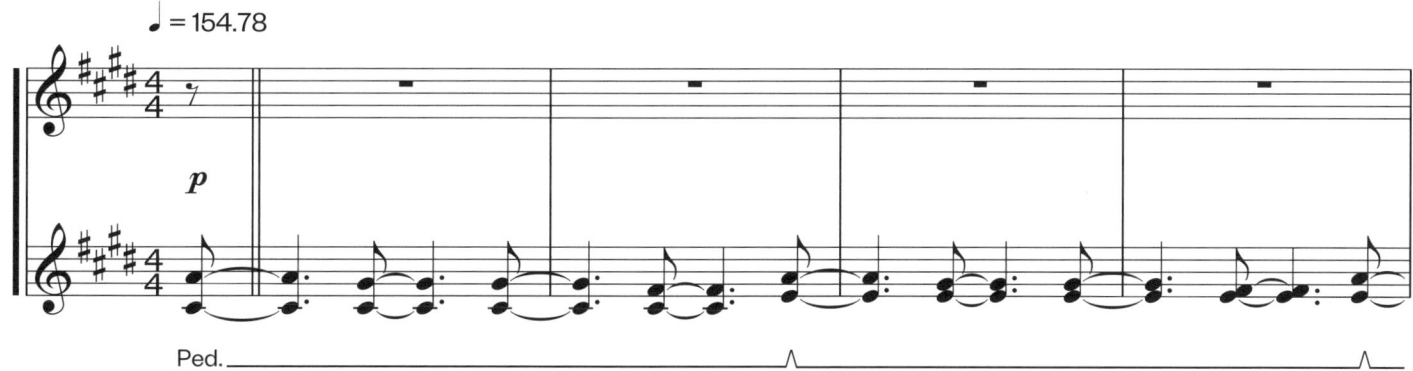

© 2007 Warner/Chappell Music Ltd
All Rights Reserved.

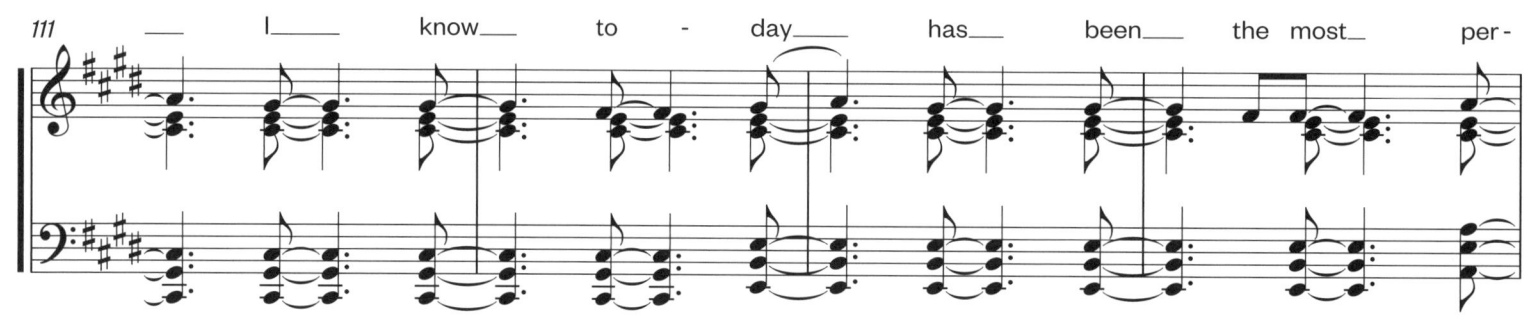

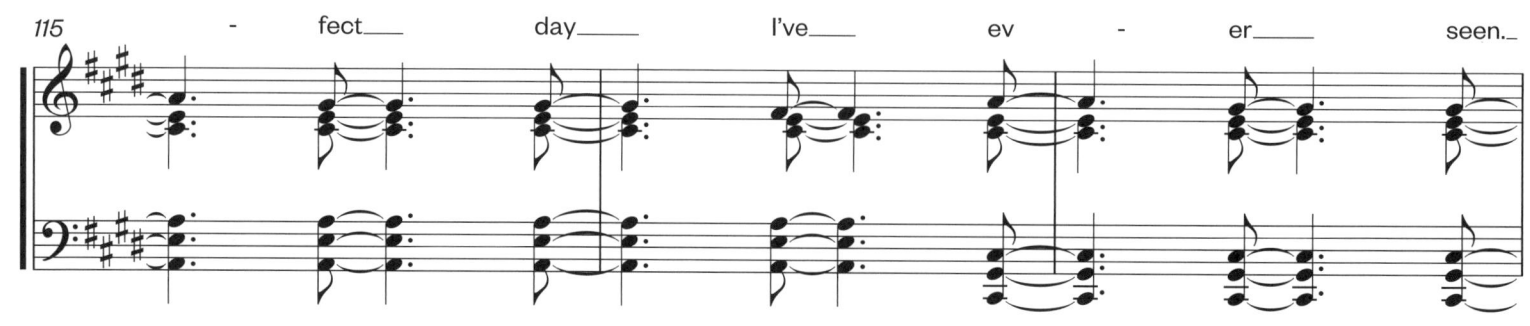

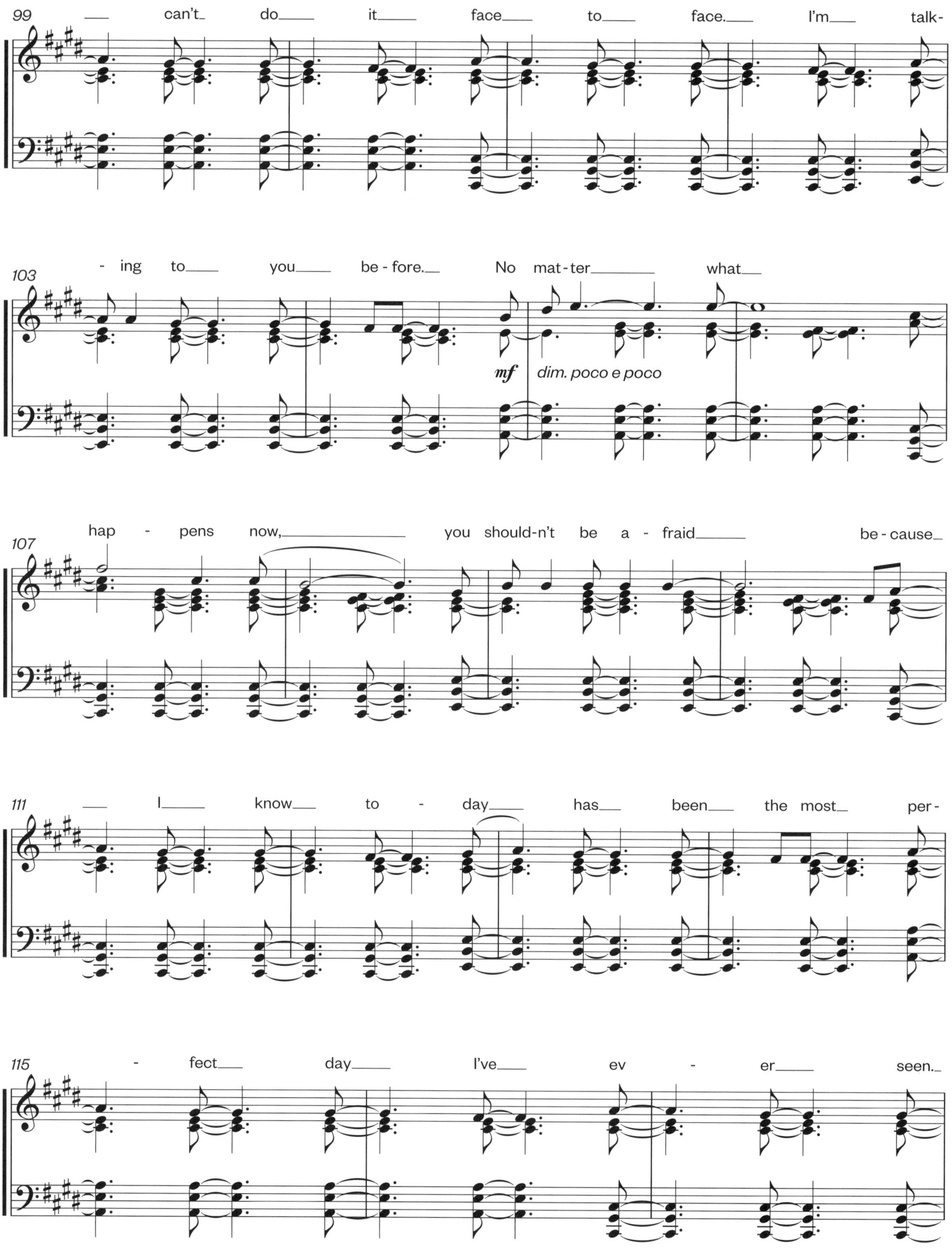
99
can't do it face to face. I'm talk-
103
-ing to you be-fore. No mat-ter what
mf
dim. poco e poco
107
hap - pens now, you should-n't be a - fraid be-cause
111
I know to - day has been the most per-
115
- fect day I've ev - er seen.

True Love Waits

Words and Music by Thomas Yorke, Jonathan Greenwood,
Colin Greenwood, Edward O'Brien and Philip Selway
Arrangement and transcription by Josh Cohen

© 2001 Warner/Chappell Music Ltd
All Rights Reserved.

INTRODUCTION TO 'PARANOID ANDROID'

I had just started my Bachelor of Music when I first met the musicians in my band Auto Luna. Pat the bassist came up to me after the first rehearsal and said, "Bro, Andy says you can play 'Paranoid Android' on the piano. Let's hear it." I nervously played my arrangement of the track for him. He paused for a few moments and then replied with a straight face, "Okay, you're in."

'Paranoid Android' is a banger. I have literally been playing variations of this track for years since my friend Nick introduced me to *OK Computer* when I was nineteen. I never managed to master it when I was younger due to the sheer complexities of reducing such an intricate song down to solo piano, but I guess that's part of the appeal of tackling such a beast. It was only in 2017, when I decided to record an arrangement coinciding with the twenty-year anniversary of *OK Computer* for my YouTube channel that I felt more confident to have another go in the ring with this track.

One of my favourite things to do on the piano is to vamp on a chord progression exploring the endless possibilities of where something so simple may go. The opening improvised theme, which was borrowed from the 7/8 section of the song eventually morphs into the first four chords of the first verse. This initial theme also provides some material for the improvised outro. As per my process when building up arrangements from scratch or previous reincarnations of a track, these sections are always evolving and changing over time.

During the process of transcribing the arrangements for this book, I did actually start jotting down some loose sketches of this track before I threw in the towel. The size of the arrangement coupled with such a feel-based improvisational approach made this song difficult to notate. It also went against the original intention of selecting only playable and accessible repertoire in this songbook. For this reason, 'Paranoid Android' was never initially intended to be included in the book. It was never played nor arranged in the moment to ever be transcribed.

In any case, my editor Lucy advised me that we should include this track in the book and I appreciate that the video was, for many of you, the first introduction to my work. As a result, this transcription was completed in a number of days by arranger guru Oliver Weeks. I am still unsure if I should be impressed with his efforts or just straight up scared.

Looking at this transcription makes me anxious. I've been struggling to even play this arrangement note-for-note myself. 'Paranoid Android' is one of my favourite songs to improvise over and whilst I never thought I'd ever see this transcription come to fruition, here it is.

Good luck. You'll probably need it.

Paranoid Android

Words and Music by Thomas Yorke, Jonathan Greenwood,
Colin Greenwood, Edward O'Brien and Philip Selway
Transcription by Oliver Weeks
Arrangement by Josh Cohen

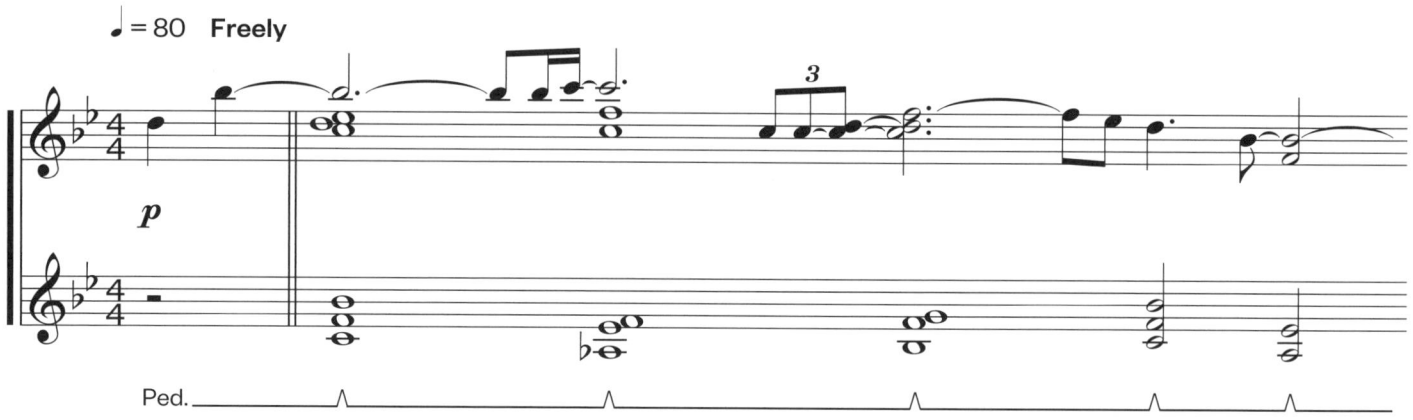
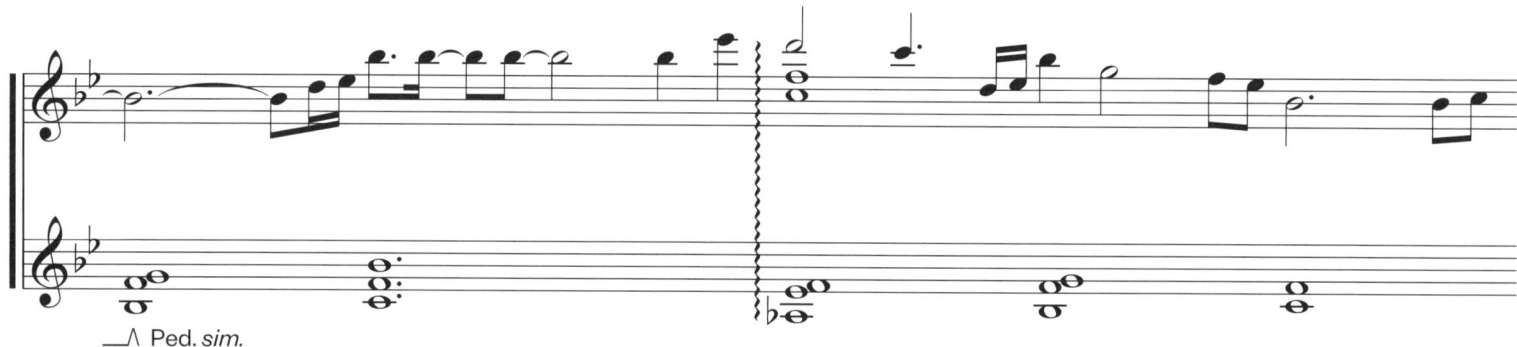

© 1997 Warner/Chappell Music Ltd
All Rights Reserved.

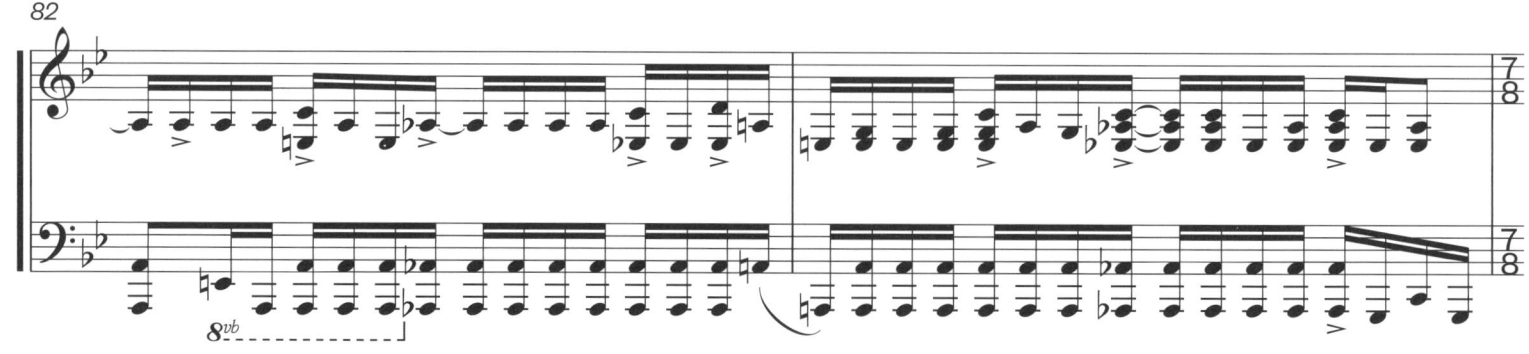